WEST MIDLANDS INDUSTRIAL STEAM in COLOUR

Part One (Non National Coal Board)

By Terence Dorrity

Copyright Irwell Press,
ISBN-978-1-906919-70-2
First published in 2014 by Irwell Press Ltd., 59A, High
Street, Clophill, Bedfordshire, MK45 4BE
Printed by 1010 Printing, China.

All the photographs in this book were taken in the West Midlands area as it was considered to be in the 1960s. This included the present West Midlands region around Birmingham and Coventry, the "Black Country" parts of Staffordshire and Worcestershire and the county of Warwickshire.

In the 1960s heavy freight trains were, at least at the beginning of the decade, still hauled by steam engines on the railway main lines. These were the lines, and in most cases the locomotives, which before nationalisation in 1948 had belonged to the competing London Midland and Scottish Railway (formerly the London and North Western Railway and the Midland Railway) and the Great Western Railway. Alongside these transport giants, and usually connecting with them, were many industrial rail systems which, because they were seen as less glamorous than their big cousins, were often overlooked despite being an essential part of the distribution network. If railways have trunk lines and branches, these were the important 'twigs' where much of the freight started and finished. In the 1960s many of them were still worked by interesting industrial steam locomotives which serviced the factories of this renowned manufacturing area bringing in the raw materials, starting the finished products on their way or shunting around the site.

This book contains a visual record of the industrial steam locomotives in use on systems other than those operated by the National Coal Board in the West Midlands in the 1960s. These were mostly 0-4-0 and 0-6-0 saddle tanks which, alongside a handful of 0-6-0 side tank engines, were built by a number of manufacturers who designed locomotives specifically for this kind of work.

I had been fascinated by steam locomotives from an early age. This probably had its origin when my mother took me to our local station at Henley-in-Arden to see the Royal Train go past. The locomotive was ex GWR 4082 "Windsor Castle". I believe this was the visit by the King, Queen and Princess Margaret to Stratford-upon-Avon on 24 April 1950, Shakespeare's Birthday. It is probable that they were not even on board at the time and that the train was on its way to Tyseley for servicing but, as I was just under four years old, it was the royal engine that impressed me. About a decade later, having made my Ian Allan book dog-eared and now armed with the indispensable Birmingham Locomotive Club pocket book of the *Industrial Locomotives of the West Midlands*, it was my father who gave me my first opportunity to photograph industrial locomotives. Although not particularly interested himself, and probably preferring to be out in the countryside, he persuaded gatemen to let us pass and patiently waited in the rain, industrial odours and grime of gasworks and factories while his young son enthused over the Bagnalls, Pecketts and Barclays puffing away on their daily duties. Thanks Dad, and thanks Mum, this book is dedicated to both of you.

Fortunately I kept detailed notes at the time I photographed the locomotives, with the aid of the Birmingham Locomotive Club's aforementioned *Industrial Locomotives of the West Midlands*. The information has been updated using the excellent Industrial Railway Society handbooks *Industrial Locomotives of the West Midlands* and *Industrial Locomotives of South Staffordshire*, both compiled by R.A. Shill. I found additional information about locomotives that have since been preserved in the web pages of the societies concerned, which are mentioned in the captions. I also found the www.warwickshirerailways site useful for background details.

Terence Dorrity, 2014.

Windsor Street Gas Works

It goes without saying that power is essential to keep the wheels of industry turning. The main sources of this power at the time, for domestic as well as industrial use, were the gasworks of the West Midlands Gas Board and the power stations of the Central Electricity Generating Board. In those pre natural gas times these relied on deliveries of coal by rail.

On Saturday 7 April 1962 "Alan", an 0-4-0 saddle tank built in 1938 by Andrew Barclay, Sons and Co Ltd of Kilmarnock (works number 2060), stood out of steam at the West Midlands Gas Board Windsor Street Gas Works, Birmingham. It was supplied new to the Birmingham Corporation Gas Department, which became part of the West Midlands Gas Board on nationalisation on 1 May 1949, and it was withdrawn from service and sent to John Cashmore and Co Ltd, Great Bridge, for scrap in July 1966. The gasworks railway was connected to an ex London and North Western Railway branch which joined the main line near the ex LNWR locomotive shed at Aston (at the time coded 21D).

Shunting at the gas works on the same day was No 3, a Peckett and Sons of Bristol "Greenhithe" type 0-4-0 saddle tank built in 1944 with the works number 2058. With its distinctive low cab, it was known as "Greenhithe", after the type, but it did not carry nameplates. Delivered new to the Birmingham Corporation Gas Department, it was one of three similar Pecketts at Windsor Street at the time and was one of last two steam locomotives there which were finally sent to John Cashmore and Co Ltd of Great Bridge for scrap in March 1969. Rail traffic continued with diesel shunters until the gasworks was closed in 1974.

Nechells East (Saltley) Gas Works

West Midlands Gas Board No 4, like No 3 at Windsor Street, was a Peckett "Greenhithe" type 0-4-0 saddle tank. Built in 1945 with the works number 2070, it was working at Nechells East Gas Works, Birmingham, on Sunday 3 November 1963. It was the only steam locomotive at this site at the time, sharing work with a couple of diesel shunters. It went to John Cashmore and Co Ltd, Great Bridge, for scrap in March 1968. The works rail connection was with the ex Midland Railway Birmingham to Derby main line at Saltley and it was called Saltley Gas Works until it was renamed in July 1963, just four months before this picture was taken. The nearby British Railways LMR Saltley depot had been coded 21A until the previous month, September 1963, when it became 2E. The gasworks was closed in 1969.

Nechells (West) Gas Works

On Saturday 7 April 1962, No 8, an Andrew Barclay, Sons and Co Ltd of Kilmarnock 0-4-0 saddle tank, was in steam at Nechells West Gas Works. Built in 1932 with the works number 1992, and supplied new to Birmingham Corporation Gas Department, it was withdrawn from service and sent to John Cashmore and Co Ltd of Great Bridge in December 1963 where it was cut up in the following month. This was one of two Barclays at Nechells at that time which worked alongside a Peckett and a Sentinel.

On the same day No 10, a 4WTG vertical boiler Sentinel, built in 1956 with the works number 9617, was also in steam at Nechells West. It was supplied new in January 1957, just two years before the final Sentinel steam locos were constructed, to Birmingham Corporation Gas Department. No 10 was an example of the more powerful 200 horsepower version of this type of locomotive. There was also a 100 horsepower version.

The following year, on Sunday 3 November 1963, No 10 was to be seen on shed at Nechells. It was sent for scrap to Cashmore's at Great Bridge in March 1968. The gas works was connected to the Birmingham to Walsall line near Vauxhall & Duddeston station and the Birmingham to Derby line at Duddeston Mill sidings. After steam locomotives were no longer in use two diesel shunters continued their work until the gasworks was closed in 1969.

No 11, a Peckett of Bristol OY class 0-4-0 saddle tank (works number 2081) at Nechells West on Sunday 3 November 1963. It was a short wheelbase version of the OY type (for the sharp curves at this site) and had been delivered new in 1947. It was relocated to the Swan Village gas works in Walsall in August 1965 where it joined a 180hp 0-4-0 diesel (North British 27544 of 1960) and performed there until the end of rail working in 1969. It was then bought privately for preservation and was moved to the Foxfield Light Railway at Blythe Bridge, Stoke on Trent, Staffordshire in August 1969.

Soho Gas Works

"Pinkney", a Peckett M5 type 0-4-0 saddle tank, at Soho Gas Works on Saturday 7 April 1962. It was delivered new to this Borough of Smethwick works which, along with the other municipal gasworks, became part of the West Midlands Gas Board on nationalisation on 1 May 1949. "Pinkney" was built in 1934 with the works number 1836. It was the only steam locomotive on site at the time, accompanied by a diesel shunter. The gasworks was connected to the LNWR main line from Birmingham to Wolverhampton but rail traffic finished at the end of 1963 and "Pinkney", named after Charles W Pinkney who perfected a gas engine in 1889 and invented a Hydrocarbon Gas Producer and a Bituminous Coal Gas Generator, was cut up at Soho in March 1964.

Wolverhampton Gas Works

On Saturday 2 November 1963, No 2 "Carbon", an 0-4-0 saddle tank built by William Bagnall Ltd of Stafford in 1902 (works no 1673) and delivered new to the Wolverhampton Gas Company was at Wolverhampton Gas Works. It was rebuilt by Bagnalls in 1943. At the time there were two Bagnall and one Robert Stephenson and Hawthorn 0-4-0 saddle tank locomotives on site along with one diesel shunter. The Stafford Road gas works was built in 1849 and later enlarged. It was close to the ex Great Western Railway Stafford Road shed (84A), which had closed just two months earlier, and its railway system was connected to both the GWR and LNWR lines.

The other William Bagnall locomotive at Wolverhampton gas works was "Victory", a newer 0-4-0 saddle tank built in 1942 with the works number 2661 and also delivered new to the Wolverhampton Gas Company. It is seen here out of steam on Saturday 2 November 1963. It is interesting to compare these two Bagnall products built forty years apart. Like "Carbon", "Victory" was scrapped in October 1965. The gasworks continued in use until 1967 when natural gas from the North Sea replaced town gas. One part of the site is now the Wolverhampton Science Park and another part is an industrial estate.

Nechells Generating Station, Birmingham

Providing electricity for the area, the Central Electricity Generating Board's two ex City of Birmingham Electric Supply Department generating stations were at Nechells and Hams Hall.

Seen on Saturday 7 April 1962, "Nechells No 1", was one of two Peckett W5 Type 0-4-0 saddle tanks in use at Nechells Generating Station in the first half of the 1960s. Built in 1916 with the works number 1438, it had been supplied new to the City of Birmingham Electric Company at Nechells. This power station replaced an earlier temporary wartime one and was opened by the Prince of Wales in June 1923. Because of this event it was unofficially called the Prince's Power Station. The larger Nechells B Power Station became operational in 1954. Rail traffic ended when the B power station closed in July 1982. It was demolished in 1988.

Almost exactly two years later, on Saturday 10 April 1965, "Nechells No 1" was still hard at work. Steam working finished when Nechells Power Station hired a diesel from British Railways towards the end of 1971. No 1, no longer required, was transferred to Northampton Power Station as a standby locomotive. In 1975 it was sold for scrap but fortunately it was purchased for preservation, first at the East Anglian Railway Museum, Chappel and Wakes Colne Station, Essex, and later at the Appleby Frodingham Railway Preservation Society at the Scunthorpe Steelworks, Lincolnshire.

No 2, the other Peckett W5 Type 0-4-0 saddle tank at Nechells, was also seen on Saturday 10 April 1965. Built in 1917 with the works number 1478, it was also supplied new to the City of Birmingham Electric Supply Department Nechells Power Station. It was transferred to Hams Hall Power Station at the start of the 1950s but had been returned to Nechells by 1957. The locomotive was scrapped in June 1972.

Standing on a turntable, an item not usually found on industrial lines because they used tank engines, on Saturday 10 April 1965 was No 3, one of two 0-6-0 side tank locomotives at Nechells. Built by Robert Stephenson & Hawthorns Ltd in 1949 (works number 7537), it was supplied new to the British Electricity Authority. These powerful side tank locomotives were needed to haul 1000 ton coal trains from the British Railways exchange sidings at Bromford Bridge, on the former Midland Railway Birmingham to Derby line, to the coal tipplers. Steam working finished in November 1971 and in the following year No 3 went to the Battlefield Line of the Shackerstone Railway Society, Leicestershire where it carries the name "Richard III".

Hams Hall Power Station, near Coleshill, Warwickshire.

Like Nechells Power Station, Hams Hall had a number of 0-6-0 side tank locomotives. On Sunday 8 April 1962 No 13, Robert Stephenson & Hawthorns Ltd works number 7846 built in 1955, was in action still sporting the pre 1958 "Central Electricity Authority" on its tank sides. Delivered new to Hams Hall, No 13 worked until 1972 when it was bought for preservation. In 1996, after spending time at various locations and gaining the name "North Downs", it arrived at the Spa Valley Railway at Tunbridge Wells, Kent, where it worked the first passenger trains on the preserved line.

On the same day a partly repainted No 5 was seen moving up to the tower to take on water. It was built in 1936 and was the sole locomotive at Hams Hall built by Hawthorn, Leslie and Co Ltd, Newcastle upon Tyne (works number 3904) before, in 1937, its locomotive building interests were transferred to Robert Stephenson & Co which built the later side tanks used at Hams Hall and Nechells power stations.

The following year, on Sunday 24 March 1963, the repaint of No 5 was complete. For a short time, from October 1954 to August 1955, No 5 had worked at Nechells. It was scrapped in late 1968. At times as many as eight of these powerful tank engines with a tractive effort of 27,000lb, of the type originally built by Hawthorn Leslie, were needed to deliver coal around the extensive rail system. There were eventually 12 of these locomotives in the West Midlands Region.

No 12, Robert Stephenson & Hawthorns Ltd 7845 of 1955, was also in action on Sunday 24 March 1963. It was delivered new to Hams Hall. There were three power stations at Hams Hall. The first station was opened in 1929, the second in 1942 and the third in the 1950s. In the 1960s the three were in full production but they have all been closed down and demolished. It is now the site of the Hams Hall Distribution Park and, in keeping with the rail theme, the Hams Hall Channel Tunnel Freight Terminal.

No 12, like No 13, was still carrying the pre 1958 "Central Electricity Authority" on its tank sides. It can now be seen on static display at the Dales Countryside Museum at the old Hawes railway station in Yorkshire. There it has been painted in British Railways lined black livery and given the BR number 67345 which originally belonged to a Great Eastern Railway class G5 0-4-4T designed by Wilson Worsdell. The real 67345 used to work on the Wensleydale line from Hawes and trains may one day again run through the station if the Wensleydale Railway project to extend to Garsdale materialises.

No 8, Robert Stephenson & Hawthorns Ltd 7067 of 1942, was working hard on the same day. The 24 March was just a few weeks after the end of one of the coldest winters on record, the Great Freeze of 1963, so Hams Hall would have been exceptionally busy rebuilding the coal stocks.

No 7 was another Hams Hall Power Station Robert Stephenson & Hawthorns Ltd 0-6-0 side tank locomotive. It was built in 1938 (works number 6965).

Also on Sunday 24 March 1963, some of Hams Hall's impressive array of cooling towers can be seen in the background behind No 10, Robert Stephenson & Hawthorns Ltd works number 7536 built in 1949.

Two years later, on a very dull Saturday 10 April 1965, No 6, Robert Stephenson & Hawthorns Ltd 6964 of 1938, was in action. No 6 remained at Hams Hall throughout its working life. It was cut up in August 1968.

Also on Saturday 10 April 1965, breaking the monopoly of the 0-6-0 side tanks at Hams Hall, No 4, a Peckett W6 type 0-4-0 saddle tank built in 1928 (works number 1738) and supplied new to Hams Hall, was shunting the wagons. Three similar Pecketts were used there. By 1968 this locomotive had been sold to a Severn Valley Railway member and it went to Bridgnorth on that railway. Later it was moved to the South Devon Railway and then to Titley Junction Station, Herefordshire where it was given the identity of No 6 "Percy", from the Thomas the Tank Engine books.

On Saturday 31 August 1968, and by then in preservation, No 4 was on show at an open day for "day members" that predated the Severn Valley Light Railway Order which was granted in November 1969. GWR 0-6-0 3205 is just behind and LMS 2–6–0 Class 2MT No. 46443 waits to leave on a train for Hampton Loade. Ivatt Class 4 2-6-0 43106 was also in steam that day. This was at the end of the very month that saw the 11 August "Fifteen Guinea Special", officially the last steam hauled British Railways main-line passenger train, and the introduction of the BR steam ban the following day.

Stewarts & Lloyds Springvale Furnaces

Elsewhere in the West Midlands, steel and tube works had their rail systems, as did other manufactures. Some of the latter were real household names: Cadbury, Dunlop and Austin among them. The steel industry is represented by two Stewarts & Lloyds sites.

On Sunday 30 September 1962, No 8 "King", an Andrew Barclay 0-4-0 saddle tank which was built in 1910 with the works number 1215, was out of use at Stewarts & Lloyds Springvale Furnaces, Bilston. "King" had been delivered new and was scrapped at the end of 1963. Like the other Barclays at Springvale, "King" had a half-cab.

Another Andrew Barclay 0-4-0 saddle tank locomotive seen that day was "Clare". Its yellow livery was showing obvious signs of the heat of the furnaces. Built in 1911 (works number 1235), "Clare" was, like "King", delivered new to the Springvale furnaces when it was owned by Sir Alfred Hickman Ltd. It was scrapped at the end of 1963.

No 12 "Victor", seen here filling up its tanks and looking a little smarter than "Clare", was another half-cab Barclay 0-4-0 saddle tank. Built in 1914 (works number 1357) and delivered new to Springvale, it was scrapped in August 1965. The works was acquired by Stewarts and Lloyds in 1921 and became part of the British Steel Corporation on nationalisation in July 1968.

"Patricia", Andrew Barclay 0-4-0 saddle tank built in 1924, was also busy about its duties on Sunday 30 September 1962. It, too, was delivered new and it was scrapped in October 1965. Steam was already on the way out at the time of this visit to the Springvale Furnaces at Bilston. The surviving steam fleet of seven Andrew Barclay and one Kerr Stewart 0-4-0 saddle tank locomotives was ranged against twelve Yorkshire Engine and two Ruston and Hornsby 0-4-0 diesel electric shunters and two Ruston and Hornsby four-wheeled diesel mechanicals, one of which was out of use.

At another part of the site on that Sunday, "Anne" was building up a good head of steam. An Andrew Barclay 0-4-0 saddle tank built in 1924, works number 1841, it was delivered new to Springvale Furnaces in October 1924 and scrapped forty-one years later. The rail system was connected to the ex Great Western Dudley to Wolverhampton line.

"Anne" was working hard that day. I saw it at work again in April 1965, just six months before it was scrapped in October 1965. Along with "Patricia", it was one of the last two steam locomotives to go. In 1954 a huge new blast furnace, replacing three smaller ones, had come into operation. Called "Elisabeth" after the daughter of the chairman of Stewarts & Lloyds Ltd, it went on to produce 275,000 tons of steel a year. The furnace was demolished in October 1980, eighteen months after steel production ended at the site.

Stewarts & Lloyds Bromford Bridge Tube Works, Erdington, Birmingham

There were three steam locomotives at Bromford Bridge Tube Works in the first half of the 1960s. In early 1962 I photographed this Peckett W6 type 0-4-0 saddle tank built in 1937 with the confusing works number 1936. This locomotive had been supplied new to the site and it was cut up there after thirty years in December 1967, just before Stewarts & Lloyds became part of the British Steel Corporation on nationalisation.

Three years later, on Saturday 10 April 1965, another Peckett, a W7 type 0-4-0 saddle tank with the works Number 2119, was out of steam. This locomotive was built in 1950 and also supplied new to Bromford Bridge. Like Peckett 1936, it was not named and was cut up on site at the end of 1967. The works exchange sidings were adjacent to Bromford Bridge station on the ex Midland Railway line from Birmingham to Derby. The railway station closed just eleven weeks after this photo was taken, on 28 June 1965.

The third Bromford Bridge locomotive on that same Saturday in 1965. This was an Avonside Engine Company SS3 type 0-4-0 saddle tank built in 1917 with the works number 1777. It had come from the Chesterfield Tube Co Ltd, Derbyshire, in 1928 and was also scrapped on site at the end of 1967. The last steam locomotive at this works, "Wellingboro No 3", a Hawthorn Leslie 0-4-0 saddle tank of 1935, arrived from Stewarts & Lloyds, Corby, in 1967 and was scrapped in 1971 leaving rail traffic in the hands of diesel shunters. The works closed in 1994.

The Austin Motor Co Ltd was putting steel to good use at the Longbridge works, Birmingham.

On Saturday 11 May 1963, the year before the ex Great Western and Midland Joint Longbridge to Halesowen branch closed, "Austin 3", a Hunslet Engine Co 0-6-0 saddle tank built in 1937 with the works number 1814, was at work. It was scrapped in March 1971 three years after Austin had become part of British Leyland. "Abernant" can be seen in the background.

Moving up to the same spot, the attractive "Abernant" was also in steam that day. An 0-6-0 saddle tank built at the Boyne Works of Jack Lane, Leeds, to the specifications of Manning Wardle in 1921 with the works number 2015, "Abernant" came to Longbridge from the Cardiff Corporation Water Department Llwynon Reservoir construction at Cefn Coed, Brecknockshire, via the dealer Thomas Ward in 1927.

Two years later, on Saturday 10 April 1965, "Austin II", a Hunslet Engine Co of Leeds 0-6-0 saddle tank identical to "Austin 3" built in 1936 with the works number 1692, was hard at work leaving the works going towards the BR sidings. "Austin II" was delivered new after an Armstrong Whitworth 0-4-0 diesel-electric locomotive was tried but not found suitable in 1933. "Austin II" was scrapped at the end of 1970.

"Vulcan", an 0-6-0 saddle tank built in 1953 by W.G Bagnall with the works number 2994, was also in action on 10 April 1965. It was one of three powerful locomotives built for the Steel Company of Wales, Port Talbot and numbered 401, 402 and 403. Displaced by diesels in September 1957, 401 and 403 were bought by Austin's and named "Vulcan" and "Victor". They had Walschaerts valve gear, self-cleaning smokeboxes, rocking grates, and mechanical lubricators. In 1973 both were bought by the West Somerset Railway and saw use in the early days of the line but, when no longer needed, "Vulcan" was moved to the North Tyneside Railway, Stephenson Railway Museum and renamed "Thomas Burt".

On the same day, but unfortunately for the purposes of a photograph, "Austin 1", an 0-6-0 saddle tank, was stabled in such a way that the only clear view was with the sun behind it. It is worth including, nevertheless, because it was one of only a very few Kitson & Co of Leeds locomotives in use in the West Midlands area in the 1960s. Built in 1932, with the works no 5459, and supplied new to Longbridge, it was purchased by the Burtonwood Brewery on behalf of the Flint and Deeside Railway Society in 1973 and re-named "Burtonwood Brewer". Later transferred to the Llangollen Railway Society, it was the only locomotive operating passenger services when the line was re-opened in 1981. It has now regained the name "Austin 1" and has visited a number of other railways including the Churnet Valley, the Chinnor and Princes Risborough and the Lavender Lines.

"Abernant" on static display at Newdigate Street children's playground in Birmingham on Saturday 10 April 1965; understandably it is looking a bit careworn since its time at Austin's only two years before. At the end of 1963 it had been sent to J Cashmore's scrapyard at Great Bridge but it was saved for the playground in February 1964. It was later removed and since 2003 has been at the Great Central Railway (Nottingham) at Ruddington, bearing the number 5 and the name "Arthur".

Cars need tyres and the best known British producer of these at the time was the Dunlop Rubber Co Ltd at the imposing Fort Dunlop factory in Birmingham. I believe this factory was at one time the biggest in the world and it was, and still is in its new retail centre incarnation, a notable sight alongside the M6. Prior to the 1970s this view was not available because the motorway had not yet been opened but the building was nevertheless very impressive.

'No 5' (it actually carried no number) shunting at Fort Dunlop on Saturday 10 April 1965. An 0-4-0 outside cylinder Peckett W4 type saddle tank built in 1943 (works number 2046) it was originally supplied to Morris Motors at Cowley, Oxford, but appropriately went from Morris Cars to Dunlop Tyres in November 1948. It was scrapped on site in September 1966 but Dunlop still used three steam locomotives, Bagnall "Dunlop No 6" and two Pecketts built in 1951; this latter pair went to Fort Dunlop in 1966 and 1967 and, like No 6, both are now preserved.

Four years later, on Sunday 4 May 1969, less than a year after the end of steam on British Railways, little "Dunlop No 6", still in industrial service, was polished up to rub buffers with the already preserved steam giants "Clun Castle", "Kolhapur", "Eric Treacy" and "Flying Scotsman" at an early Standard Gauge Stream Trust open day at Tyseley, Birmingham. Built in 1941 (works number 2648), No 6 was one of a batch of nine 28-ton 0-4-0 saddle tanks built by William Bagnall for the Ministry of Supply Royal Ordinance factories. It was converted from oil to coal firing and sold to Dunlop in 1966. After withdrawal in 1971, it spent some time at the Battlefield Line at Shackerstone, Leicestershire but since 2008 it is to be found on the Chasewater Railway, Staffordshire, where it now carries the name "Linda".

Metropolitan-Cammell, Washwood Heath, Birmingham.

An overcast moment at Metropolitan-Cammell, Washwood Heath on Saturday 10 April 1965 throws S1045, an Andrew Barclay 0-4-0 saddle tank built in 1938 (works number 2052) into shadow. Carrying the stencilled number but no name, this locomotive had been "Metro-Cammell" when supplied new to the site. It was scrapped in September 1965. The two gas holders in the background were right beside the now demolished Nechells B Power Station. The ex Midland Railway Birmingham-Derby line ran between the power station and Metropolitan-Cammell. Just out of the picture to the right were two vast cooling towers. It is now the site of the Star City entertainment complex.

Cadbury Brothers, Bournville, Birmingham

Inside the engine shed at at Cadbury's Bournville factory on Monday 9 April 1962, and not in use that day, were two of the fleet of four steam locomotives at that time. "Cadbury No 1", an Avonside 0-4-0 side tank locomotive built in 1925 (works number 1977) and No 9, a Hunslet of Leeds 0-4-0 side tank built in 1949 (works number 3665). Both were delivered new to Bournville. No 1 was withdrawn from service in 1963. No 9, particularly interesting because it had Walschaerts valve gear, was scrapped on site in March 1966.

Outside on the same day, and looking good enough to eat in its appropriate milk chocolate livery, "Cadbury No 6", an Avonside Engine Company 0-4-0 side tank built in 1923 with the works number 1921, was hard at work. No 6 was supplied new to Cadbury. In January 1964 it was sold to J.Round Ltd Metal Merchants of Wednesbury, where it was scrapped in 1967. The Cadbury rail system operated until 1976.

No 10 was also at work; the last new steam locomotive to be purchased by Cadbury's, it was one of the last Pecketts to be built. It was an OY2 type 0-4-0 saddle tank built in 1955 with the works number 2156. In March 1963 it was sold to the National Coal Board and moved to Tilmanstone Colliery in Kent. It later went to Chislet Colliery, also in Kent where, in 1965, it was observed in an unusual silver livery which was, perhaps, an undercoat. It has since been scrapped.

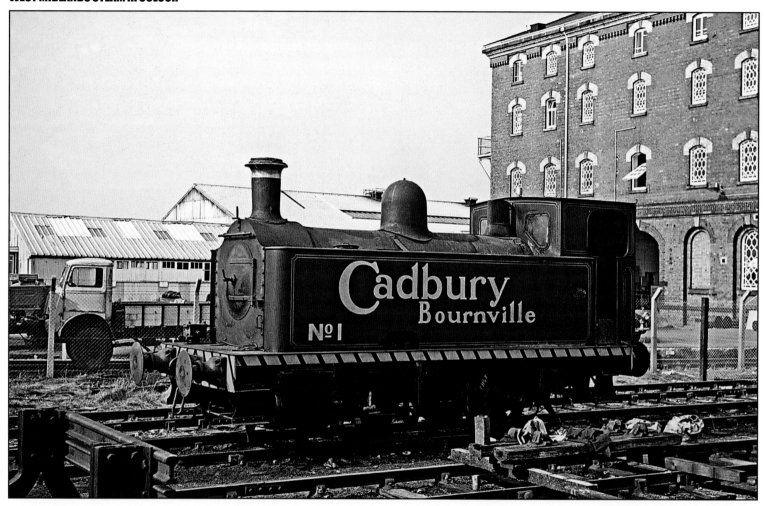

On Saturday 30 March 1963, just a year after it was seen on shed in the earlier photograph, "Cadbury No 1" was sitting outside in the sunshine at the Dowty Railway Preservation Society site at Ashchurch, Gloucestershire, where it had arrived only a month before. At this time the Cadbury steam fleet had been withdrawn and rail traffic at Bournville was in the hands of four North British 0-4-0 diesel hydraulic locomotives which had been delivered in pairs in 1959 and 1961. In 1983 it was moved to the Gloucestershire Warwickshire Railway at Toddington, Gloucestershire, where it was the first steam locomotive to operate passenger trains on the line the following year. It is now at the Birmingham Railway Museum, Tyseley.

Alders Paper Mill, Tamworth

Of the many smaller factories using steam locos, Alders Paper Mill at Tamworth was of special interest through of the presence of 1340 "Trojan", seen here on Sunday 24 March 1963. This 0-4-0 saddle tank was built by the Avonside in 1897 (works number 1386) and belonged to Messrs Dunn & Shute of Newport Town Dock until, in 1903, it was purchased by the Alexandra Docks Railway, Newport, which was then absorbed into the Great Western at the grouping in 1923. Sold to the Netherseal Colliery, Burton-on-Trent in July 1932, it was re-sold to Alders in 1947. Now preserved in GWR livery, "Trojan" has been based at the Didcot Railway Centre, Oxfordshire, since 1968.

Only two locomotives were used at Alders (Tamworth) Ltd. As well as "Trojan" on Sunday 8 April 1962 there was an out of steam Andrew Barclay 0-6-0 saddle tank (built 1918, works number 1576). It did not carry a fleet number. Note the spark arrester, surely an essential accessory for work in a paper mill. Originally at Nobell's Explosives Co Ltd, Pembrey, Carnarvonshire, where the spark arrester would have been even more necessary, this locomotive was bought from R H Neal of Park Royal, London, in 1927.

Two years later, on Thursday 2 April 1964, the Barclay saddle tank was in steam. Alder's railway line, which linked the paper mills with the LNWR Trent Valley Line at Coton Crossing, was closed in 1967 and Barclay 1576 scrapped on site in February 1968, four months after rail traffic had ceased. The paper mill was demolished at the turn of the 20th century, after about 200 years of production, and housing now occupies the site.

Rugby Portland Cement Works, New Bilton

In Warwickshire, but well away from the West Midlands conurbation, there were several cement works with rail systems. In the middle of the decade steam was still in use at the Rugby Portland Cement Works at New Bilton, near Rugby. On Wednesday 27 October 1965 No 5, an 0-6-0 saddle tank which was delivered new to New Bilton in 1948 from Robert Stephenson and Hawthorns Ltd of Newcastle upon Tyne (works number 7387), stood forlornly out of steam in the rain. It is likely that this locomotive did not work again as it was scrapped just five months later in March 1966.

On the same dismal day, No 1, a relatively rare 4WTG Sentinel of Shrewsbury built in 1953 with the works number 9559, was in steam at New Bilton. It had arrived a year earlier from the company's Tottenhoe Quarries, Dunstable, Bedfordshire. In 1967 this locomotive went to Thomas Hill Ltd, Killamarsh, Yorkshire and a year later to R Y Pickering & Co Ltd, Wagon Works, Wishaw, Lanarkshire, where it continued in use until the 1970s. It is now preserved on the Tanfield Railway, near Gateshead, Tyne and Wear, to where it was moved in 1979.

On Wednesday 2 February 1966 an 0-6-0 saddle tank built in 1926 by Manning Wardle (works number 2047) was hard at work at New Bilton. 2047 is notable because it was the last locomotive to be built by the Manning Wardle Boyne Engine Works, Leeds, which went into liquidation in 1927. It was ordered by Rugby Portland Cement in April 1926 and delivered in the August that year.

With the cement works in the background, 2047 is seen backing up its load of wagons. After it was withdrawn from service, the locomotive was moved to the Severn Valley Railway for preservation and named "Warwickshire". At first it was painted blue and later it was returned to green. It even has the honour of having a 7mm kit-built Agenoria '0' Models version. This picture poses the intriguing question: "How many men does it take to change a lightbulb?"

Associated Portland Cement Manufacturers Ltd Harbury Cement Works

Not very far from New Bilton was the Associated Portland Cement Manufacturers Ltd Harbury Cement Works and on Tuesday 6 April 1965 0-6-2T 6697, from Leamington Spa shed, was delivering a rake of wagons to the exchange sidings next to the GWR Birmingham-Paddington main line where the cement works shunter "Cunarder" was waiting. 6697 was withdrawn only a year later, at the end of May 1966, from Croes Newydd shed, Wrexham, the last of the class to be taken out of service. Bought by the Great Western Society in 1966, it arrived at the Didcot Railway Centre in 1970.

A few minutes later "Cunarder", a Hunslet 0-6-0 saddle tank built as one of a batch of six (works number 1690) in 1931, took over the recently delivered train. It was supplied new to the contractors building the King George V dock at Southampton, which explains its name. In 1933 it was moved East for construction work on the Dover train ferry dock. In 1935 it was moved again to continue its seaside life at Wallasey on the sea wall and promenade contract there. After use on further construction projects, "Cunarder" was sold and started work at Harbury in March 1957. When no longer required there it was moved for preservation to the Quainton Road Society, Buckinghamshire, in April 1969. Since then it has been at a number of sites including the Swanage Railway, where it was rebuilt with side tanks, painted black and given the BR identity of scrapped Derby built LMS Fowler Dock Tank 47160. Its most recent move was to a site near Poole for restoration.

War Department supply depot, Long Marston

Long Marston, in deepest rural Warwickshire far from the West Midlands factories, where the 154 Railway Operating Company Royal Engineers had a supply depot, on Tuesday 20 August 1963. WD 0-6-0ST 155 was standing in steam outside the Nissen hut style engine shed; it was built by Robert Stephenson & Hawthorns Ltd of Newcastle in 1944 with the works number 7143.

WD182, a Vulcan Foundry of Newton-Le-Willows example of the Hunslet austerity design built in 1945, works number 5273, was transferring a train from the ex GWR main line. This locomotive had originally carried the number WD 75283.

Some variety from the standard War Department austerity Hunslet type 0-6-0 inside cylinder saddle tanks, of a design introduced in 1943, was provided by an operational steam crane that day. The austerity saddle tanks are often called J94s by enthusiasts because this was the class designation given by the LNER to a batch of 75 of them that became part of their motive power fleet the year after the end of World War Two. This is the site of the new Long Marston Military Railway centre project.

Two years later and Long Marston, now under the newly created Ministry of Defence, seemed to have become a preparation point for the sale of locomotives to other concerns. On Sunday 1 August 1965, WD 144, a 1944 built William Bagnall 0-6-0 saddle tank (works number 2746), stood between WD 143, another Bagnall (2740 of 1944), and Hunslet built WD 134 polished and on parade waiting to be redeployed. WD144 went to see action at the Prince of Wales colliery, Pontefract, and WD 143 at Ackton Hall Colliery, Featherstone, both in the NCB Yorkshire Area.

WD 134, originally numbered WD 75118, was built by Hunslet in 1944, works number 3168. After a spell at Bicester Central Workshops, Oxfordshire, it took a detour via Long Marston when it was sold to the National Coal Board and sent to Primrose Hill Colliery, Woodlesford, in the North Yorkshire Area. It was later transferred to Wheldale Colliery, Castleford, where it worked until the early 1980s. Now preserved, it can be seen at the Embsay & Bolton Abbey Steam Railway in North Yorkshire and it has been named "Wheldale" after the last colliery where it worked.

By the 1960s narrow gauge steam was a rare sight in the West Midlands but two examples of locomotives which were no longer at their original sites are shown here and on the following page.

On Sunday 26 April 1964, 2 "Lady Luxborough", a William Bagnall 0-4-0 saddle tank built in 1919 (works number 2088), sat on the drive of the very non-industrial site of Oldberrow Vicarage Rectory, near Henley-in-Arden, Warwickshire. This was one of a pair of two foot gauge Bagnall locomotives originally ordered by the Ministry of Munitions but delivered new to the Birmingham, Tame and Rea District Drainage Board at Minworth when not needed at the end of the First World War. No 2 went to Oldberrow in 1961 and was given its name. It was shown at fetes and fairs but later sold on. In 1991 it was acquired by the Bredgar and Wormshill Light Railway in Kent and given its originally intended, but never carried, name "Armistice" and the number 4. Its sister, No 1, Bagnall 2087 of 1918, was preserved at the Birmingham Museum of Science and Industry and given the name "Leonard". When the museum closed, "Leonard" was moved to the Abbey Pumping Station industrial museum, Leicester.

Looking rather sorry for itself, on Wednesday 11 August 1965, "Mesozoic", an 0-6-0 saddle tank built by Peckett & Sons, Bristol, in 1913 (works number 1327), stood rusting in the yard of P. Fenwick & Co Ltd. St James' Works, Brackley, Northamptonshire where it had been since July 1961 when the site was run by E L Pitt & Co (Coventry) Ltd. It originally worked on the 1ft 11½in gauge system of the Rugby Portland Cement Co Ltd at Southam Works, Warwickshire. It was one of six similar Pecketts and a Bagnall 0-4-0 saddle tank which were all delivered new to Southam. There were also several petrol and diesel driven locomotives there. Four of the Pecketts were preserved. "Mesozoic" is now to be found at the Bromyard and Linton Railway, Herefordshire. The other two were scrapped as early as 1943.